THE EASTER STORY FOR CHILDREN

Written by
MAX LUCADO, RANDY FRAZEE, AND KAREN DAVIS HILL

Illustrated by
FAUSTO BIANCHI

ZONDERKIDZ

The Easter Story for Children
Copyright © 2013 by Max Lucado, Randy Frazee, and Karen Davis Hill
Illustrations © 2013 by Fausto Bianchi

Requests for information should be addressed to:

Zondervan, *Grand Rapids, Michigan 49530*

ISBN 978-0-310-73594-6

Editor: Mary Hassinger
Art direction: Kris Nelson
Design: Cindy Davis
Illustrator: Fausto Bianchi, represented by Beehive Illustration
Artwork colorist: Steve James

Printed in the UNITED STATES OF AMERICA

17 18 19 20 /OPM/ 22 21 20 19 18 17 16 15 14 13 12 11 10 9 8 7 6 5 4

For our grandchildren—

*"Write these things for the future so that people
who are not yet born will praise the Lord."*

Psalm 102:18 **(NCV)**

—The Authors

Jesus was a very busy man. He worked hard to spread the Word of his Father and how much God loves his people.

Jesus' ministry had grown strong. His disciples loved him. The people gathered in great crowds to hear him preach. They loved him too.

But not everyone was a follower of Jesus. Some people were not sure about what he said. Some priests were angry because Jesus claimed to be the Son of God. Some rulers were not sure what Jesus meant when he talked about a kingdom.

Jesus knew then that it was time for his work and time on earth to be over.

As Jesus and his twelve disciples sat around the table to share the Passover meal, Jesus told his friends this would be their last meal together and that a difficult time was coming.

Then he took a loaf of bread, blessed it, tore it in pieces, and shared it with everyone at the table. Jesus told them that the bread was like his own body that would be given for them. "Eat this to remember me," he said.

Jesus took a cup of wine, blessed it, and shared it with the disciples. "This cup of wine is a reminder of my promise to be your Savior," he said.

Then Jesus told them something that made them very sad. "One of you will turn against me and will give me to my enemies."

"Is it me?" each one asked.

"I would never do that," Peter protested.

Jesus said, "Peter, I'm sorry to tell you but, before morning, you will deny you know me—three times—before the rooster crows!"

Later that night Jesus walked to the Mount of Olives where there was a peaceful garden. He knelt down and prayed to his Father in heaven. He asked God to give him the courage to face the troubles ahead.

When his prayer time was over, Jesus rejoined the disciples. Suddenly a crowd of angry men showed up— the high priests, temple police, and leaders. One of Jesus' disciples named Judas Iscariot was with the bad men. He walked over to Jesus and kissed him. (That was the signal to the leaders that Jesus was the one they wanted to arrest.) Judas was the traitor!

Rattling swords and marching feet
broke the quiet in Jerusalem that night.
Soldiers and temple leaders hustled
Jesus through the dark, sleeping city.
They had Jesus tied up. They were
taking him to see the city leaders, those
people who did not like Jesus and
his messages of love.

Each time the soldiers and Jesus turned a corner, Peter darted behind a building. *What are these soldiers going to do to Jesus? Where are they taking my Lord? If they see me, will they arrest me too?* Peter wondered.

The soldiers pushed Jesus through a gate and into the courtyard of the house where the high priest waited for the prisoner. Peter was close enough to watch and hear what was about to happen. He sat near the fire where others had gathered.

Peter pulled his robe over his head, hoping no one would see his face.

A servant girl recognized Peter. "You're with him!" she said, pointing to Jesus.

"No, no. I don't even know that man," Peter lied.

The soldiers began to make fun of Jesus, hitting him and treating him badly.

A soldier sitting near Peter said, "Aren't you one of his disciples?"

Peter said, "I don't know what you're talking about."

The high priest began asking Jesus questions. Jesus answered, "Everything I've done has been out in the open for all to see. I've taught and ministered, but not in secret. Why are you treating me like this?"

Just then a soldier noticed Peter near the fire. "I saw you in the garden with Jesus! You are one of his disciples," he said.

Peter denied it. "Not me," he said. Then the courtyard rooster crowed his morning call. The sound of the rooster reminded Peter of Jesus' words. "You will deny me three times before the rooster crows." Peter ran out of the courtyard. He cried and cried, disappointed with himself for not being true to Jesus.

People packed the streets of Jerusalem to look at Jesus. The word was all over town: Jesus had been condemned to die. He had been beaten, spit on, and made fun of. Now the soldiers whipped him, forcing him to march to the place where he would be executed.

The followers of Jesus wanted him saved from the terrible punishment. Men shouted, women cried, children were sad and upset.

In the middle of all the turmoil, Jesus struggled under the heavy wooden cross he was forced to carry. There was nothing anyone could do.

The soldiers pounded huge nails through the hands and feet of Jesus into the cross. They raised the cross, with Jesus on it, and stuck it in the ground. There Jesus hung for hours, in great pain. Two criminals hung on crosses next to him.

Many people who loved Jesus were there for him. But many other people made fun of Jesus as he suffered. "If he's the Son of God as he says, let him save himself," they laughed. One of the criminals made fun of him, too. But the other criminal believed Jesus was God's Son. "When your kingdom comes, will you save me?" he asked Jesus. And Jesus promised to save him.

The painful punishment continued for hours. Jesus' mother and disciples watched, filled with sadness at his suffering. Soon the sun stopped shining. Darkness was all around. Then Jesus cried out, "It is finished," and he died.

Friends of Jesus took his body and buried it in a tomb.

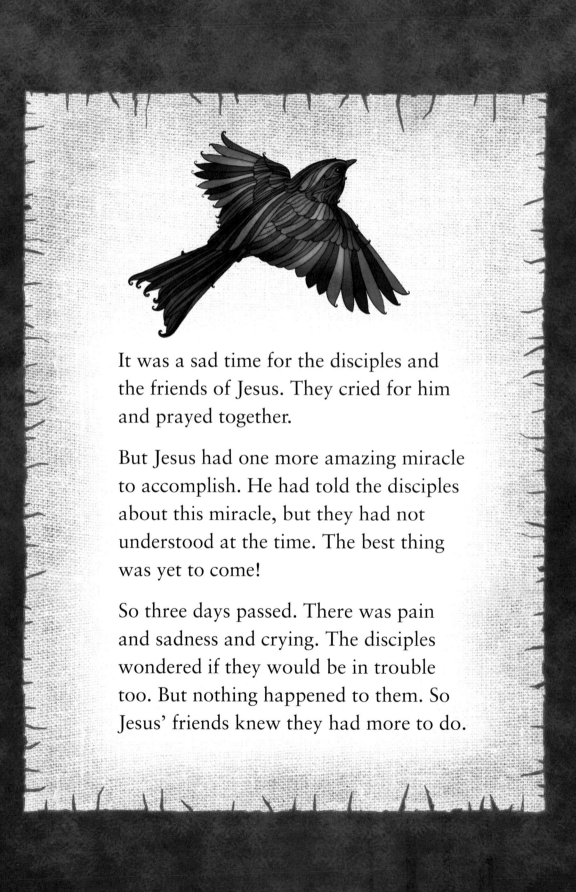

It was a sad time for the disciples and the friends of Jesus. They cried for him and prayed together.

But Jesus had one more amazing miracle to accomplish. He had told the disciples about this miracle, but they had not understood at the time. The best thing was yet to come!

So three days passed. There was pain and sadness and crying. The disciples wondered if they would be in trouble too. But nothing happened to them. So Jesus' friends knew they had more to do.

At that time, when someone died, the women poured good smelling oils on the body and wrapped it in a nice burial cloth.

So Mary Magdalene, Salome, Joanna, and Mary, James' mother, headed for the tomb on Sunday morning to take care of Jesus' body. On the way, they began to talk about the tomb and what they would do when they arrived. "Who will roll away that big heavy stone for us?" one of the women asked.

But when they arrived, the stone had already been moved from the tomb's entrance. Mary Magdalene ran ahead and peeked inside.

"He's gone!" she shouted. "Our Lord is gone! Look—the burial garments are still here, neatly folded up!"

"Don't be afraid," spoke a calm, quiet voice from the tomb. Mary Magdalene looked again and saw an angel.

"I know you're looking for Jesus. He's not here. He was raised from the dead, just as he promised. Now go and tell the others he is risen," the angel said.

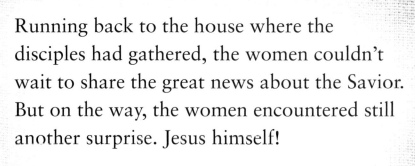

Running back to the house where the disciples had gathered, the women couldn't wait to share the great news about the Savior. But on the way, the women encountered still another surprise. Jesus himself!

"Good morning," Jesus said as he smiled at his friends. "Lord!" the women cried joyfully, dropping to their knees and worshiping the Son of God. "Go tell the others I'll meet them in Galilee," Jesus said.

The women got up and did as Jesus told them. "The Lord is risen!" they said over and over again as they hurried to meet the disciples and share the amazing news.

Later, the disciples argued about and discussed Mary Magdalene's remarkable news. "I saw Jesus raised from the dead!" she had told them over and over.

As they talked about this wonderful news, Jesus suddenly appeared in the locked room. The disciples were shocked. The last time they saw him, he was dead!

"Peace be to you," Jesus said. He showed them the nail scars on his hands. He showed them the side of his body that had been cut by the soldier's sword.

When the disciples realized the person in front of them really was Jesus, they were very happy! Mary had been right! And Jesus was happy to be with his friends again. He gave them a special blessing and told them he had a big job for them to do.

Jesus explained to the disciples, "I want you to tell everyone about the blessing that I came to give: forgiveness and life eternal for everyone who believes in me. Soon the Father will send the Holy Spirit to help you and give you strength and power."

Though the disciples didn't understand everything, they understood Jesus had done what he said: he had died and was alive again. The disciples knew they had been chosen to do an important job.

And what a job they had to do! But they were not alone. The disciples had Jesus with them for a little while longer. Jesus continued to teach them and spend time with them and then, one day, he went up to heaven.

For awhile after Jesus left them, his followers stayed together and prayed. They waited in Jerusalem for the power of the Holy Spirit to come. They had no idea when this would happen or what it would be like, so they prayed and gave thanks until it was time.

The Holy Spirit came just as God promised, through his Son. The Spirit's comfort brought them peace. The Spirit's power filled them with courage. The disciples were able to perform miracles in God's name. And they went out to tell the world that the Messiah had come.